unds and Sights
of
Taos Valley

by Helen G. Blumenschein

Sounds and Sights
of
Taos Valley

Text and Illustrations
by
Helen G. Blumenschein

Edited by Marcia Muth Miller

the sunstone press

Santa Fe, New Mexico / June, 1972

Copyright © 1972 by Helen G. Blumenschein

Printed in the United States of America.

All portraits by Helen Blumenschein are done in
charcoal and red conté except
that of Mr. Sharp which was done in pencil.
Laura Gilpin photographed all of the author's
drawings except where otherwise noted.

FIRST EDITION
2,000 Copies

1SBN 0-913270-04-0

Library of Congress Catalog Card Number: 72-84251

Printed by Starline, Albuquerque, New Mexico

ACKNOWLEDGEMENTS

For the last twelve years I have been indebted to Jack Boyer, Director of the Kit Carson Museum in Taos, New Mexico, to Dr. Myra Ellen Jenkins, State Historian, State Record Center, Santa Fe, New Mexico, to Eleanor B. Adams, Albuquerque, New Mexico, for her help in the translation of the 1694 De Vargas Journal, as well as to all the librarians of northern New Mexico.

Also, my thanks to Mrs. Ruth Marie Colville of Del Norte, Colorado, for her help in the location of the 1694 campsites in the De Vargas route through Colorado, to Dr. Bertha Dutton, Director of the Museum of Navaho Ceremonial Art, Santa Fe, New Mexico, who gave an adult class in archaeology, and later, on techniques at the Pot Creek Ruin, and to Orval Shreeves of Taos for his invaluable knowledge of the whereabouts of pithouses and trails.

The author accepts full responsibility for all her conclusions on historical research.

Helen G. Blumenschein

Dedicated To All The Young People Of Taos Valley Who
Are The Vanguard Of The Future

Who shall make the river flow or
Stop its course toward the sea?
However great the universe, the skies,
However deep and dark the secrets of the earth
Feel not alone — oppressed by fate
But search the joys, the sorrows
For the gate to understanding.

Helen G. Blumenschein

Sounds in Taos Valley

Some indicators of the inevitable change that has come to the Taos Valley are found in the sounds. From the very beginning, these sounds meant comfort to the weary traveler who came into the Valley in search of food and shelter. While it is true that now it is the sound of trucks and automobiles instead of horses, the promise of needed sustenance and a place to stay are still present in a beautiful environment.

The Stone Age "tourist" in the Taos Valley must have found the sounds of pounding mortar and pestle most satisfying since he had an empty stomach after his long trek through the wilderness.

Later, the grinding of stone-against-stone was the sound that greeted the traveler as locally-grown corn was ground throughout the fertile Taos Valley. The American soldiers who came in 1847 were supplied with flour by the many small double-stoned grinding mills scattered along the valley's numerous rivers.

By the late 1800's, sounds of grinding stones were changed to grinding gears as two modern mills were built in the Ranchos Plaza, one by Alexander Gusdorf and the other by Squire Hart.

In the early 1900's there was the putt-putt of still another mill, Ben Randall's, which stood opposite a lovely willow tree. The mill was fed by a spring. (The spring at the south entrance to Taos Plaza has now been bulldozed flat and holds a "Kentucky Fried Chicken" stand!) In addition to supplying the mill with needed water power, the spring provided water for the early settlers until they completed their own hand-dug wells.

It is said that some of the Taos Indian women slipped away at night to have their corn ground in the Hondo Valley rather than kneel for hours grinding it on their stone *metates*. The machine age had brought changing times.

Water in the area's many native trout streams has always provided a source of pleasant sound in the valley. These streams, splashing down toward the Rio Grande Gorge, are hosts to mallard ducks who dive beneath their waters for succulent plants.

At Taos Pueblo after 1629 the sound of mission bells pealed forth every day until the 1800's when the Pueblo mission was abandoned and then replaced by Guadalupe Church at Taos Plaza. Soon too, the sound of horse

TAOS PUEBLO, SOUTH SIDE, 1929. Photograph by Laura Gilpin.

hooves accompanied the creaking of wagons as people came to sell, trade and buy at market. There was also the pounding of hooves from the racetrack. And at night, the music of the *fandangos* in town could be heard, accompanied by whoops and cries of men who drank at the many bars and watched the twirl of the roulette wheel.

The distilleries were introduced at a time when the beaver trappers were avid customers. Bars still abound and contribute a major source of income to the people of Taos Valley.

Today the tourist hears the roar of trucks since Taos fears a by-pass to the west which would drain the flow of visitors away from the plaza area.

No longer do Catholic church and chapel bells ring out to lure the worldly into their sanctuaries. Now there are more art galleries than bars, and there are motels galore. Or, if you prefer, you can take your camper into the Carson National Forest where you will hear only an occasional sonic boom from a jet passing overhead, a poor competitor to the small brook tinkling by your side and the raucous camp robber bird in a nearby tree.

In the 1890's when the search for gold finally reached the Hondo Canyon twenty miles northeast of Taos, another sound reverberated through the thin atmosphere. An Englishman named Twining had brought in a big machine which shook like a palsied hand as it sifted sand and stones into a large vat of water and chemicals.

Picks struck frantically at stone; tunnels were driven into the Sangre de Cristo mountains. Today *that* kind of gold rush is over, and on these same mountain slopes the sound is softer but no less sweet to entrepreneurs — the swish of skis against snow.

Springtime, and in particular, Eastertime, has always had its own special sounds in the Taos Valley. Some of these are now not so easily heard, but they are still there for the attentive ear!

During Easter week, mingled with the piercing cry of the coyote on a moonlit night, comes the equally sad wail of a *Penitente* flute leading processions of devout men singing their way to and from *moradas*.

After Easter Week come the nerve-wracking winds of spring, blowing dust and fine sand against the windowpanes, shrieking down the stovepipes and whispering gossip in one's ear.

The winds die down; the snows melt on the mountains, feeding the streams that plummet toward the Rio Grande Gorge, hastening in their pursuit to the Gulf of Mexico.

The sun hits the top of Taos Mountain at dawn, and the early risers at the Pueblo make plumes of blue smoke curl from their chimneys. The meadowlarks sing, announcing the arrival of spring.

On the third of May the drums beat at the Pueblo. All is ready for the relay race of young men and children. Their young bodies are painted

Aerial view of Taos Pueblo, 1970. This photograph taken by Peter Dechert — courte *School of American Research.*

according to their clans. Most of them are barefoot; there are sparse amounts of eagle down glued to their bodies, and a piece of yucca is tied around one ankle. Several older men along the track utter shouts of encouragement — ò-mo-pah (run — run)! Their mothers, dressed in their finest white buckskin boots, laugh and call out to their young ones to run — run! The thud of their small bare feet, moving faster and faster on the ground, the clear light of early morning — everyone is happy. The race does not last long. The relay racers now collect in two parallel lines facing each other, while a male chorus chants to the beat of a single deep drum. They separate and go to the underground kivas.

Spring is here!

IN MEMORIAM — Long-suffering and hard workers, the burros brought firewood from the mountains for the poor folks who had no wagons. When were they introduced from Mexico?

*WINTER — HONDO VALLEY. Brush, ink and gouache drawing.
Courtesy Gallery A, Taos.*

The town of Los Cordovas on the Taos Creek several miles before the creek enters a gorge and falls headlong into the Rio Grande (formerly called the Rio del Norte). It is located on State Road 240, three miles west of Ranchos Plaza. This was the original crossing of the Taos Pueblo River in 1540-41 and 1598-1600, when Alvarado and Oñate came to visit the Taos Pueblo. At this place, only one crossing of a river was necessary to reach the pueblo.

A PRIVATE CHAPEL IN PLACITA — *one-half mile north of Taos Plaza on Highway 3 to Colorado.*

NUESTRA SEÑORA de DOLORES — one of the many old chapels in the little villages around Taos. Vespers, 7:00 p.m. September 14. Mass, September 15. Two miles east of Taos near entrance to Taos Canyon, Highway 64.

CHAPEL AT LLANO QUEMADO. The old altar was purchased by the Museum of New Mexico.

View from the top of the Picuris Saddle where the original Camino Real entered the Taos Valley. The present U.S. Vista Lookout is four miles east of this point connected by a delightful dirt road winding through the pines of the Carson National Forest. By following the boundary fence and moving northward, you will have walked to Talpa.

In the distance at the foot of their Sacred Mountain nestles the Taos Pueblo with the Pueblo River running through it to the Rio Grande. Its source: Blue Lake. Far to the northwest on the horizon line looms a 10,800 foot volcano, San Antonio.

History

Tourists have been coming to Taos for millenniums. Even early man, like the modern fisherman, delighted in its many rivers rushing westward to the Rio Grande Gorge. An abundance of wild game once filled the stomachs of hungry travelers, although much of that early food source has been depleted.

Bands of Indians supposedly came in migratory waves from Asia via the Bering Straits during the warmer cycles of climate in that area thousands of years ago. Perhaps some bands came from Central America; or perhaps the arid country to the south of Taos deterred them. More exact proof is still needed.

A Pinto point site dating from 3000 BC is the earliest evidence of man in the Taos area. However, near Albuquerque the pages of history were turned back thousands of years more with the discovery of the Sandia points. It seems reasonable to assume that Taos Valley with its many attractions drew man before 3000 BC.

The climate must have been colder than it is now because hundreds of pithouses similar to underground kivas presently used at the Taos Pueblo for religious purposes have been found all over the valley. Later the Indians built above ground in the Taos Valley during periods which archaeologists call Pueblo II Period and Pueblo III Period.

What happened to these early Indian inhabitants I hope does not happen to us. There was a heavy increase in population, followed by a 22-year drought (1277 to 1299 AD). The climate became colder and the growing seasons shorter. It is not known whether the Indians began fighting among themselves for food or whether they were invaded by other hungry tribes from Mesa Verde or Chaco Canyon. But all that remained of these Taos Valley Indians by 1540 when Captain Hernando de Alvarado was sent north from the present Coronado State Monument area by Coronado was Taos Pueblo. The Indians whom Alvarado found were adorned with turquoise which they had mined (a commercial turquoise mine is still in operation on Highway 142 in Colorado). On the earliest maps of the 1500's Taos Pueblo is shown as "Taosjii" or "Taosii."

Over the years many *conquistadores* came to see Taos Pueblo. Its structure, three stories high and topped by drying racks, was as imposing then as now, and its trade fairs were famous. Taos became the northern trading center of the pueblos and the breadbasket of the west during the 1800's.

Because it was impossible to get into the valley during the winter months, Taos continued to be an isolated community since the Picuris Mountain formed a barrier at right angles to the Sangre de Cristo Range straight down to the Rio Grande River.

Taos was not reached by the illegal Spanish *entradas* from 1560 to 1592. However, the Pueblo was not able to escape Spanish rule or religious domination.

Colonial policy of Spain during the conquest of Mexico and New Mexico in the Sixteenth Century, until 1598, was carried on by cruel, rich *conquistadores* who paid for their own expeditions and in return expected to find gold and slaves.

These *conquistadores* had just finished a passionate religious war against the Moslems and Jews and had run them out of Spain. Now they turned to the conquest and Christianization of the New World. Only Catholics were allowed to settle in the New World, and until 1692 they attempted to make Catholicism dominant over the native Indian religions.

In 1598 Don Juan de Oñate declared a halt during his march forty-seven miles southwest of Taos at San Juan Pueblo. In 1610 the settlers from San Gabriel established their capital at Santa Fe under Governor Don Pedro de Peralta because they were fearful of the Indians around them in the Española Valley.

The Pueblos were not happy or at peace because of Spanish infringements on their freedoms. The Indians organized under the leadership of a San Juan Indian named Popé who later moved to Taos Pueblo. On August 10, 1680, they revolted, striking down all but two of the priests. The missions were vandalized. After a confrontation at Santa Fe the settlers were allowed to flee to El Paso.

In 1692 another rich military man, General Don Diego de Vargas, arrived with a new order of colonial policy from Spain. His entry into Santa Fe was one of the most successful bloodless conquests in history. De Vargas brought settlers to Santa Fe in 1693, although few of the original inhabitants who remembered the Pueblo revolt would return. He established another villa at Santa Cruz in 1695 and visited Taos Pueblo three times — 1692, 1694, and 1696.

De Vargas brought no revenge to the pueblos, but he did demand that their inhabitants be re-baptized. In turn he promised to protect them from the Plains Indians. This combination of professional diplomacy and military ability enabled him to start the trend toward friendly trade relations with the Pueblo Indians. There were only four abandoned haciendas in the valley when De Vargas came in 1692.

As for the Indians, they had finally realized that they could not fight European guns with bows and arrows. They were willing to compromise by adding the Catholic religion to their own. By staying on reasonable terms with the conqueror they were able to keep their villages intact.

On his third expedition in 1696, De Vargas was presented with a gift by a Taos Indian, an oil painting of *Nuestra Señora de Aranzazú* from the Basque Country of Spain. It had been saved from the Pueblo Mission church. The church was built in 1629 and was first abandoned in 1640 when some of the Taos Indians fled to Kansas after having killed their priest, Fray Miranda, in 1639. Others went there after the 1680 revolt when they again assassinated the priest at the Pueblo Mission church.

During the period of living together after the reconquest by De Vargas the Indians taught the Spanish to raise corn, squash, chili and beans, while the Spanish conquerors contributed guns, horses, cows, sheep and wheat to Indian culture. With the straw from this wheat the Spaniards taught the Indians how to make adobe bricks in rectangular forms. Before this the Pueblos had been pouring the mud in much the same way in which we pour concrete, using ashes as a binder for the sticky mud. It is the Spanish who were responsible for the fireplace and the beehive-shaped ovens.

The few settlers who came to Taos Valley after the reconquest lived near the Pueblo Mission Church, outside the wall on the southwest side. As their population increased, they spread out in various directions — in 1760 to the Ranchos Valley, and then in 1815 to Arroyo Seco, Valdez and Arroyo Hondo.

The Spaniards participated in the famous Indian Fairs at Taos, and many of them settled in the Ranchos Valley along the Las Trampas River, now called the "Little Rio Grande." The problems that began during the movement of Spanish settlers into the area are still subjects of current controversy. The Cristobal de la Serna Grant was licensed in 1710, but it was never occupied by its owner. It was sold in 1724 to the Don Diego Romero family and it remains in that family although it has been in litigation for many years due to debts to the Weimer family. These old titles are still causing numerous headaches to Taos Valley residents, and a solution must soon be found.

A major Indian attack on Taos settlers had occurred in 1760 when a thousand Comanches raided the Villalpando hacienda, only two miles from the Pueblo, then continued on raids throughout the area. More than 40 Spanish women and children were kidnapped and many Indians were killed in this attack.

Despite the Indian threat, settlers began farming the Ranchos Valley about 1760. After receiving a license to build the present Ranchos church in 1801, they constructed a plaza and fortified it with towers as protection against the annual attacks by the Plains Indians.

During the 1790's some Ranchos settlers requested the Taos Indians to allow them to move closer to the Pueblo. The plaza for the village of Fernando de Taos was formed, enabling the settlers and the Indians to unite forces in driving off the frequent attacks by invaders from the Plains. Governor Juan Bautista de Anza had issued a proclamation urging the settlers along New Mexico's many streams to solidify their positions around a walled plaza to protect themselves as the Pueblo Indians did.

According to the Fernando de Taos Land Grants, Taos Plaza was built between 1796 and 1798. Because the Indians had allowed settlements on what was Indian land grant property, later to become reservation land, it wasn't until 1926 that clear title to Taos Plaza was settled.

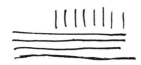

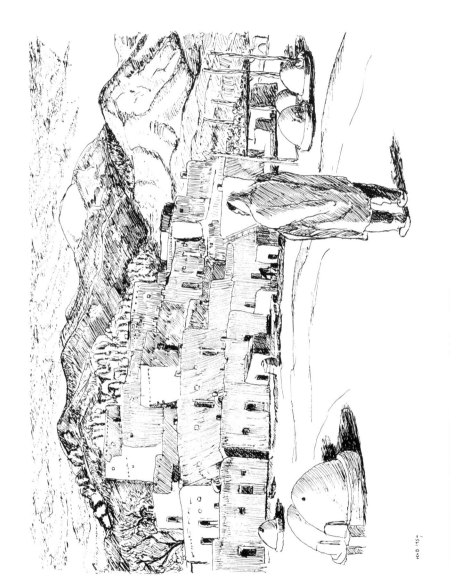

NORTHSIDE TAOS PUEBLO — pen and ink — 1950.

The Pueblo Indians became completely Christianized by the 1700's through the work of the Franciscan Friars.

MANUEL LUHAN, Taos Pueblo, 1939. He is one of the present Taos Pueblo Council members and was a former governor. Photographed by John Collier, Jr. from a drawing by Helen G. Blumenschein.

JOHN CONCHA, 1949, late Taos Pueblo Council member and former governor.
Photographer unknown.

Telesfore R. Romero

"Hunting Grouse"
by
Helen G. Blumenschein Taos 1952

TELESFORE R. ROMERO, 1952. Interpreter for the Pueblo prior to World War II. He is still active in Pueblo affairs.

ELIZA M. ROMERO, 1945. Wife of Telesfore Romero and daughter of Council Member Jim Mirabal. Photographed by Shaffer's Studios from a drawing by Helen G. Blumenschein.

MANUEL SUAZO, 1942, a Taos Indian. Photographer unknown.

BARBARA LUHAN, 1949. A wise, kindly face of Taos Pueblo. Photographer unknown.

CRUZ ROMERO, 1948. One-half Ute Indian and one-half Taos Indian. The Utes were a tribe who once inhabited the San Luis Valley and sporadically attacked Taos Pueblo. One of the Utes' most famous chiefs, Ouray, was born in Taos Pueblo. Laura Gilpin photo.

JUAN JESUS MARTIN, 1958. Taos Indian said to have lived more than one hundred years.

This was the only natural spring between Antonito, Colorado, and the Ojo Caliente River, at Tres Piedras. Not only did the Indians camp here, but also De Vargas on his way south to Santa Fe in 1694, and De Anza on his way north to ambush the Comanches in 1779. Two years before the railroad came to Tres Piedras, the stagecoach stopped here too. The present caretaker of this spring used to sell arrowheads to the passengers on the D & R G Railroad, which came from Antonito, Colorado, in 1880 to Embudo Station on the Rio Grande. Ruth Marie Colville discovered this historic site (1969) and took this particular photograph.

MATILDA LUHAN, 1956. An unusual Taos Indian Pueblo face.

Indian Children's Games.

A Taos Indian Fireplace at the Pueblo.

In 1803, under the leadership of President Thomas Jefferson, the United States signed the Louisiana Purchase agreement with Napoleon Bonaparte of France, making the Arkansas River the northern boundary line of New Mexico although it had not yet been surveyed.

Lt. Zebulon Pike was sent west to identify the Louisiana Purchase southwest boundaries in 1806. A book written by Pike was followed a year later by a more complete one on the explorations of Lewis and Clark who had been sent by President Jefferson to study and establish the northwestern boundaries of the Louisiana Purchase.

These books generated interest among easterners, and restless settlers began to move westward as "Manifest Destiny" became the settlers' credo.

The revolutionary spirit of the late 1700's in Europe permeated the New World, and in 1821 Mexico broke from Spain to become the Republic of Mexico.

New Mexico suffered from this break. Unreasonable taxes were levied. Mexico's land division policies were questionable, and they still pose problems for surveyors. The Maxwell Land Grant is the most famous example of disputes arising from greed and poor surveys.

In 1837 José Gonzales, whose mother was a Taos Indian living in Ranchos Valley, became Governor of New Mexico for a short period after the assassination of Governor Albino Pérez in Santa Fe. Governor Gonzales was killed a short time later by Manuel Armijo who came north with his own army and established himself as governor of New Mexico. Time was running out for the Mexican rulers, however. In 1846 the United States declared war on Mexico and sent Stephen Watts Kearny to head the western march. Armijo offered no resistance to Kearny's army. Kearny named Charles Bent, a famous Taos trader, as civil governor of New Mexico, and continued on his march to California. Not all the inhabitants were satisfied with this easy surrender to the Americans. A group of Indians and their Mexican allies decided to revolt. Governor Bent and others were marked for assassination.

Governor Bent left Santa Fe at Christmastime, 1846, to visit his family in Taos. He had been warned that an attempt would be made on his life, but he chose to ignore it. He reached Taos safely, but on January 19, 1847, he was scalped and killed at the door of his Taos home.

The angry Mexican-Indian mob that killed Bent and several others in Taos continued to Turley's mill ten miles north and killed seven Americans there. There was more killing too at Mora east of Holman Hill.

Although it was deep winter, soldiers led by Colonel Sterling Price traveled over Picuris Mountain to defeat the rebels. Colonel Price, Captain Burgwin and Colonel St. Vrain, with 479 men and a single cannon, marched on Taos and fought the main battle at the mission church in Taos Pueblo.

After two days' siege the Indians and their Mexican allies surrendered to Colonel Price when he pierced the walls of the abandoned church which had been pressed into service as a fort. The thirty U.S. soldiers killed in the battle were buried in Cementario Militar, renamed a few years later the "American Cemetery," and still later, the "Kit Carson Cemetery."

Kit Carson, Charles Bent's brother-in-law, was in California at the time of Bent's assassination and was therefore unable to help in negotiations. The homes of Bent and Carson are both public museums now, and Carson is buried in the ground that bears his name.

Col. John C. Frémont in December 1848 was snowed in with his expedition at Camp Desolation high in the San Juan Mountains northwest of Del Norte, Colorado. On this Fourth Expedition Col. Frémont was searching out a route for a railroad line across the southern Rocky Mountains — in midwinter! A detailed account of Frémont's last expedition can be found in *The Men And The Mountains*, by William Brandon.

All mules in camp had frozen to death and had been eaten while the army waited for a terrible snowstorm to cease. In desperation Col. Frémont told his troops, "Every man for himself," and they began a weary walk from their "Christmas Camp," 110 miles to the nearest help — Questa, New Mexico.

There were several scattered groups, and a few men who were with Frémont and Alexis Godey were left behind upon reaching Questa. Godey and Frémont got horses and continued on into Taos.

Frémont went at once to Charles Beaubien's store. Kit Carson, famed scout on previous Frémont expeditions, and Bill Owens were there. He limped up to them but was so emaciated and drawn that he was not recognized until he spoke.

The next day Godey returned to Questa with food for the half-frozen men left behind. He continued backtracking the east side of the upper Rio Grande with supplies and fresh horses until he picked up the starving groups of the Fourth Expedition scattered along the route. Eleven men had died of starvation and cold.

On February 11, 1849, Godey and the remaining men returned to Taos, and Frémont left Taos two days later for California. He arrived in time for the Gold Rush, and became a millionaire 18 months later. He soon became one of California's first two senators.

Bill Williams, guide of the Fourth Expedition, was sent with Benjamin J. Kern to pick up the cache and valuable papers which the expedition had been forced to leave behind. Williams and Kern were never seen again.

An authentic biography of a famous Taos Valley resident is long overdue. Padre Antonio José Martinez, who was born in Abiquiu, New Mexico, founded the first private school in Taos. He was a dynamic man filled with a new spirit, and had studied for the priesthood in Durango, Mexico.

When the French Bishop Jean Baptiste Lamy was sent to Santa Fe in 1850, he started to tax the residents in order to modernize the church. Few chose to fight the powerful bishop, but Padre Martinez did not hesitate to speak his disapproval of increased taxes. Not only did he refuse to obey the bishop, but he also wrote denunciations of Lamy. As a result of this and his illegitimate children, the padre was excommunicated. This action did not deter him, for he continued to preach from his own chapel.

Martinez brought a printing press to Taos where he published books for the school which he had founded. He even went so far as to print political pamphlets and was a member of the Legislature for many years.

Padre Martinez is buried in the Kit Carson Cemetery. The Spanish tribute carved on his headstone reads, "The Legislature of New Mexico called him at the time of his death, The honor of His country."

The battles of the Civil War were never waged closer than 100 miles from Taos, and only one incident left its mark on the memory of that valley. The Union Flag was flown over Taos Plaza twenty-four hours a day following an attempt to tear it down during the height of the Civil War. The flag was nailed to a pine tree by Captain Smith Simpson, Kit Carson and Colonel Ceran St. Vrain. Some of the men posted themselves in a store on the plaza and guarded the flag day and night so that no further attempts could be made to tear it down. Today it is still flown around the clock.

When the Territories of Arizona and Colorado were annexed to the Union (1861 and 1863), the Territory of New Mexico was drastically reduced in size.

A gold rush in Colorado in the 1860's brought many people to Elizabethtown in the Moreno Valley by the 1880's, and some of them spilled over to Red River to the north. Gold was mined in the Red River country until the boom ended in 1893. (Today we watch in dismay as the Molybdenum Mine in the Red River recreation area tears down a whole mountain. While it lasts the mine supplies work for 500 men, but what will happen after the mountain is gone?)

For a brief period of 60 years (1900-1960) Taos was to know peace and quiet.

MOTÉ, DEMOSTHENES MARTINEZ, 1939. He worked for the Blumenschein family for some years before joining the army in World War II. Photographer unknown. From an oil by Helen G. Blumenschein.

GABRIEL JEANTETE, 1947. Took over Moté's job with the Blumenscheins. His fine sons are now important businessmen in the Taos Community. Photographed by Shaffer's Studio, Taos, from a drawing by Helen G. Blumenschein.

JOSÉ JEANTETE, Jr., 1951. A nephew of Gabriel Jeantete. This family is descended from French trappers who came to Taos in the early 1800's.

EMELIA
by Ehen G. Blumenschein

EMELIA MONTOYA. Cook for Mabel Dodge Luhan, later served the Blumenschein family for 12 years.

RAY ARCHULETA, 1956. Formerly a farmer, he now works for the Molybdenum Mine. Mr. Archuleta also helped the young people in the digging of the pithouses during the 1950's.

There was another kind of excitement. At the close of the mining boom a small, energetic young artist appeared on the scene. Joseph Henry Sharp was commissioned by the Smithsonian Institution to paint Indians before they all disappeared from the United States. Sharp was so delighted by what he found in the Taos Valley that he returned to his studies in Paris with glowing reports of the area. He urged two fellow students, Ernest L. Blumenschein and Bert Phillips, to come and see for themselves.

The two artists, then in their early twenties, were not at all familiar with camping, guns or horses, but they bought a "surrey with a fringe on top" in Denver and bumped their way south in 1898. Although they were actually headed for Mexico City, they became so enthralled with Taos that they went no further. The two men spent their lives painting the people and the mountains of the Taos area while they urged other artists to share their good fortune.

The Taos Society of Artists was formed in 1912 and remained active until 1927 when all eleven of the founders became financially independent. Founders included Catharine Critcher who remained for only a year, later settling in Washington, D.C.

New Mexico gained statehood in 1912, entering the Union with Arizona. Once a part of New Mexico Territory, Arizona had requested its separation during the time of the Civil War. Colorado had also taken a 50-mile chunk of New Mexico when it became a territory in 1861. It became a state in 1876.

Two World Wars came and went, leaving abandoned homes in the Taos Valley when many families left to make their living in California. Couples from the East came to replace them, however, and for 20 years displacement and replacement kept the population constant.

By 1968 another culture, the "hippies," had entered the Taos Valley. These young people, moving in large numbers (most of them from California), came in search of a new Shangri-la.

The way of life of the Taos Indians began to change too. The Pueblo's population increased from 400 persons in 1900 to 1,470 by 1968. The Indians saw the Sangre de Cristo Mountains become a ski center, and they watched the Pueblo's sacred religious area, Blue Lake and its surrounding wilderness, become the envy of recreationists.

Following 50 years of pleas from Taos Pueblo and Spanish and Anglo friends, Congress granted title-trust for the 48,000 acre wilderness to Taos Pueblo on December 15, 1970. The acreage had been used previously by the Indians on a 50-year "terminal lease" in Carson National Forest. In August 1971 Taos Pueblo observed an enormous feast-day. The Pueblo was opened to the public. The Indians barbecued two buffalo from their own herd and fed the hundreds who came into the Pueblo for the two-day celebration.

This has had to be a condensed and brief history and was taken from the author's two-volume history of Taos now being completed.

MR. AND MRS. E.L. BLUMENSCHEIN, photographed by Paul Thompson of New York City, shown working together in the Sherwood Studios after their return from Paris where they were married in 1905. Mrs. Blumenschein was the former Mary Shepard Greene. Their studio was located just above the studio of E. Irving Couse, Sr.

JOSEPH HENRY SHARP, 1947. First came to Taos in 1893. He painted Indian heads for the Smithsonian Institution.

O.E. BERNINGHAUS, 1948. A painter from St. Louis, highly successful and loved by the community. His designs for floats of the "Veiled Prophet" parade in St. Louis were famous. Photographer unknown.

Frieda Lawrence

by

Helen G. Blumenschein 1947

FRIEDA LAWRENCE, 1947. Wife of D.H. Lawrence, a perfect foil for a tubercular poet and genius in the use of English prose.

DOROTHY BRETT, 1941. The last member of the D.H. Lawrence circle, herself an original painter of Indian subjects. Lady Brett was brought to the United States by the Lawrences and is now an American citizen.

ANDREW DASBURG, 1958. An internationally-known artist and follower of Cézanne who taught art in his early years. He still lives and works in his studio at Talpa.

EULALIA EMETAZ, 1939. She started "La Galeria Escondida," one of the first successful art galleries in Taos. Taos has some fifty galleries in the summertime.

FRANK WATERS, 1947. He has helped the Indians tremendously through his writings, the most famous being The Man Who Killed The Deer, *published by the Swallow Press, Chicago. Photographed by Shaffer's Studio, Taos, from a drawing by Helen G. Blumenschein.*

MRS. ALEXANDER GUSDORF, 1940's. After her husband's death she became the head of the First State Bank of Taos. An early pioneer from Germany, her two daughters were born at Ranchos de Taos. One grandson, Melvin Weimer, survives.

*EYA FECHIN, 1948. Daughter of a famous Tartar Russian portrait painter who came to
Taos in the early 1920's. Eya's mother wrote a delightful reminiscence of pre-World War I
Russia,* The March of the Past. *Eya became head of a school for modern ballet in
California.*

Helen Wurlitzer
by
Helen G. Blumenschein

HELEN WURLITZER, 1950's. Formerly of Cincinnati, she was a true patron of the arts who lived her last years in Taos and founded the Wurlitzer Foundation which is still active.

SPUD JOHNSON, 1947. Author, poet, and rebel from California in the early days. His own hand-printed Horse Fly *became famous as well as his later columns in the* Taos News *and* The New Mexican. *Photographer unknown.*

Archaeology

Archaeology, one of my hobbies, played a role in aiding Taos Valley economy and preserving information on the early settlements in the area.

In 1950 Dr. Bertha Dutton was persuaded by twenty archaeology enthusiasts in Taos to give a ten-lesson course which started a group of us digging at the Pot Creek ruin. The area was owned by Ralph Rounds who later established the Fort Burgwin Research Center. The ruin and Research Center (headed by Dr. Fred Wendorf) has been transferred to the Southern Methodist University in Texas. The Fort Burgwin Museum is on Highway 3.

Three years later, Orval Shreeves pointed out a pithouse to me in the Hondo Valley. This was confirmed by Mr. Stanley Stubbs of the Laboratory of Anthropology in Santa Fe. With his advice and financing from Mrs. Thomas Curtin and Mr. and Mrs. Boaz Long, youngsters from the Taos Valley were paid to dig out five pithouses on what was then Chilton Anderson's property. I kept records of the activities, supervised and worked on the project. Dr. Jerry Brody of the University of New Mexico in Albuquerque, assisted by 60 students, continued our work and finished excavating the pithouses in Hondo Valley as well as new ones near the Lawrence Ranch.

A little later Dr. Herbert Dick, now of Adams State College in Colorado, headed the digging at Picuris Pueblo, about a mile north of Highway 75 in the Peñasco Valley. Picuris Pueblo is of the same language group (Tiwa) as Taos Pueblo. Student archaeologists under Dr. Dick were allowed to excavate the refuse pile at the pueblo, and their findings indicated that Picuris had its beginnings in 1150 AD.

Today visitors are guided through these excavated ruins by Picuris Indians, and a museum was constructed recently to display various findings from the digs as well as crafts from Picuris Pueblo.

Picuris had an added inducement to visitors — two trout-filled lakes which await the angler. A fee is charged.

The Taos Indians became interested in the material found in these excavations, and information concerning the Pueblo of Taos was made available through the research of Dr. Florence Ellis, Professor of Anthropology, University of New Mexico, and Dr. Myra Ellen Jenkins, then Senior Archivist, State Record Center, Santa Fe. They were expert witnesses for the Pueblo of Taos, U.S. Indian Claims Commission in the case of "Pueblo of Taos Versus the United States."

Some artifacts taken from the Hondo Valley pithouses and the Pot Creek ruin are on display at the Kit Carson Museum in Taos, courtesy of the Laboratory of Anthropology in Santa Fe.

From Left To Right — Mrs. Gene Hodge, Mrs. Curtin (the children's patron), Miss Elizabeth Roy, and Dr. Fred W. Hodge. This picture was taken at Hondo Valley, 1955, by the author.

SPANISH-AMERICAN CHILDREN — digging in a pithouse in the Hondo Valley. This dig was subsidized by the Laboratory of Anthropology, Museum of New Mexico, through the generosity of Mrs. Thomas B. Curtin and Mr. and Mrs. Boaz Long. Here: two young helpers and a culinary jar they found under a floor.

Epilogue

Taos Valley, like the rest of the nation, is undergoing a radical change. The landscape and those who people it are changing. These drawings show the degree of change. The strong faces, like the strong mountains, were recorded before they were stripped by the erosion of time and neglect.

The faces of now are not those of yesterday — look about you.

Today more of us are slowly *beginning* to think in terms of the earth and how to save it from destruction.

The Indians have been living *with* nature for hundreds of years, to a point we have not reached — allowing only the fittest to survive at birth. They have gone beyond us in psychology and treat the insane with respect and kindness, as though they have a spiritual power the average individual does not. In some of the Indian religions the initiate is sent out alone, to fast and seek a vision before he is again received into his clan. How far ahead of us they really are!

The Spanish-American of Taos (and I am not speaking of the Chicano from California or Mexico) has a long history of survival despite astonishing odds. He was neglected by his feudal landowners, forgotten by his mother country, and used by his elected politicos.

There was land-grabbing by both the Mexican Republic during its brief 25 years of rule and by the first reckless young American settlers who dashed westward in search of gold.

The gold-seekers found gold and took it, but they also took lumber from forests, birds from the fields, and they called the predatory animals "evil" and killed them by trap or poison — forgetting or ignoring the balance of nature.

The Taos Indians saw the encroachments on their land by recreation seekers, and saw how their fellow tribesmen to the south fell victim to easy dollars by giving 99-year leases of their reservations.

The peace and quiet in the Taos Indians' wilderness area, on a 50-year "terminal lease" from the Carson National Forest, was attractive to the outsider.

The small lakes, set like gems in the glacial peaks of the Sangre de Cristo Mountains, were and are looked upon with covetous eyes by our latest class in society, the well-to-do, restless sun-seekers. The Taos Indians have had to unite to preserve their land and their heritage.

World War II sent many of our Taos Valley men to the only U.S. anti-aircraft unit in the Philippines. Soon they became POW's for the duration. Ambitious Spanish-Americans went to California for good wages and jobs. Two thousand left Taos County, and the vacuum was filled by a new kind of American who came to escape the hectic city life. Many retired couples also came. All enjoyed the art colony atmosphere and the almost foreign quality of the *adobe* houses. (This was before the houses became stuccoed, before subdivisions were laid out, and before the state complained about the town's sewer.) As a result of "progress," the small mountain streams were polluted by more and more septic tanks, more people and more building.

Just how much growth and progress can Taos Valley take? Arizona is already calling for subdivision controls. Ranchos Valley is protesting the building of the Indian Camp Dam. A land grant dating from 1710 and 1725 has been cut into strips of just a few feet in width because the owners willed it to their children in equal portions while family members kept increasing.

The only solution is to cooperate, tear down the fences and farm the whole area for mutual benefit. But will the people of Taos Valley do it? It is more likely that they will sell to trailer courts, to subdividers, to the lumber men who are happy to cut Picuris Mountain to pieces, or to the miner who might strip it!

There was a road spoken of by Governor de Anza in his 1779 military journal as the "Camino Real." It is four miles west of present U.S. Hill on Highway 3.

A hot springs area lies idle in Miranda Canyon because no one can clear the title. Another one on the Rio Grande is in the same state and for the same reason. Yet, a Mr. Wombley had a toll bridge and hot mineral bath stopover for a stagecoach from the Denver and Rio Grande train in the 1890's! Later, John Dunn built a toll bridge road four miles further north where the Hondo joins the Rio Grande. Today a few avid fishermen swarm in the summer months to this junction, and a few hippies wander in ecstasy among the lava rocks, sunning and swimming.

It is a shame that more of this region's history is not taught in our local schools.

Where do we go from here?

In 1970 the first sign of wisdom came from the government when it returned the 48,000 acres of leased Carson National Forest land to Taos Pueblo. Let us hope the United States government keeps that trust and does not allow another recreation lake such as Cochiti Lake Dam with its subdivisions on any other reservation.

Now the government wishes to help the Spanish-American with the Indian Camp Dam east of the Ranchos Valley. The history of these people has always been tragic, and so they trust no one, neither their politicians nor the government.

If America can learn from its own history where it succeeded and where it failed to solve public relations and environmental problems, there is hope for the future.

Taos Feast Day Dates

JANUARY 1	Turtle Dance about 2:00 p.m. Also: social dances at irregular intervals throughout the month, all at Taos Pueblo.
JANUARY 6	Deer or Buffalo Dance at Taos Pueblo.
APRIL 1	Blessing of the Animals, 2:00 p.m., Ranchos de Taos.
MAY 15	San Ysidro Feast Day at Los Cordovas — Blessing of the Fields — No longer takes place.
JUNE 13	San Antonio Feast Day on La Loma in Taos.
JUNE 24	San Juan Day Corn Dance. Corn Dances at irregular intervals throughout the summer at Taos Pueblo.
JULY 25-26	Corn Dance at Taos Pueblo. Afternoon.
JULY 25-26	Taos Fiesta, timed to coincide with July Corn Dance.
SEPTEMBER 14	Procession, 7:00 p.m. at Cañon Chapel, Nuestra Señora de Dolores.
SEPTEMBER 29	Sundown Dance at Taos Pueblo (around 4:00 p.m.)
SEPTEMBER 30	San Geronimo Fiesta. All day at Taos Pueblo.
OCTOBER 3	Firelight procession at 6:00 or 7:00 p.m. at Ranchos Church. Vespers in honor of St. Francis of Assisi.
OCTOBER 4	Saint Francis of Assisi Feast Day at Ranchos de Taos.
NOVEMBER 1	All Saints' Day at Taos Pueblo.
NOVEMBER 2	All Souls' Day at Taos Pueblo.
DECEMBER 8	Feast Day of Immaculate Conception. Upper Ranchitos.
DECEMBER 11	Firelight procession. Vespers at Our Lady of Guadalupe Church, Taos Plaza ... rebuilt after a fire in 1962. Originally built about 1803, it had a tin roof and steeple added in 1912.

DECEMBER 12	Feast Day of Our Lady of Guadalupe at Taos Plaza.
DECEMBER 24	Christmas Eve procession at Taos Pueblo, sometime after 4:00 p.m.
DECEMBER 25	Deer Dance at Taos Pueblo about 2:00 p.m. or Matachinas Dance (of Mexican origin) which lasts for two or three days.

Interesting Sources of Information
on Taos Valley

Adams, Eleanor B. (editor, translator, annotator) *Bishop Tamaron's Visitation To New Mexico. Journal of 1760.* Historical Society of New Mexico Publications in History, February 1954. (This work available at libraries.)

Adams, Eleanor B. and Fray Angelico Chavez. (translated and annotated) *Missions of New Mexico 1776.* (The Journal of Fray Anastasio Dominguez describes the trip from Santa Fe to Taos and return.) University of New Mexico Press, 1956. (This work available at libraries.)

Brandon, William. *The men and the Mountains:* Morrow & Company, 1955. (Frémont's fourth expedition which ended at Taos.)

Bunting, Bainbridge. *Taos Adobes.* University of New Mexico Press and Fort Burgwin Press. 1964.

Cather, Willa. *Death Comes For The Archbishop.* 1967. Reprint. Knopf, New York.

Curtin, Leonora S.M. *Healing Herbs of the Upper Rio Grande.* Laboratory of Anthropology (Santa Fe, New Mexico) 1947. Reprinted by Museum of the Southwest, Los Angeles, 1965.

Davis, W.W. *El Gringo, or New Mexico and Her People* (1854). Reprints: Rydal Press, Santa Fe, New Mexico, 1938, and Rio Grande Press, Chicago, Illinois. 1962.

Dutton, Bertha. *Let's Explore Indian Villages, Past and Present.* Museum of New Mexico. 1970.

Espinosa, Manuel J. *First Expedition of De Vargas into New Mexico. (1692)* In Vol. 10 of "The Coronado Series." George P. Hammond, editor, University of New Mexico Press, 1940.

Fergusson, Erna. *New Mexico, A Pageant of Three People.* Knopf, New York City, Second Edition. 1964.

Forrestal, Peter P. (translator). *Benavides Memorial of 1630.* Academy of American Franciscan History, Washington, D.C. 1954.

Gregg, Josiah. *Commerce of the Prairie.* University of Nebraska Press, Lincoln, Nebraska. 2 Vols. Reprint. 1967.

Hammond, George P. and Agapito Rey. *Don Juan Oñate, Colonizer of New Mexico 1595-1628.* University of New Mexico Press, Albuquerque, New Mexico. 1953.

Harmsen, Dorothy. *Western Americana.* Northland Press. 1971. Editor, Dorothy Monthan. (There are 18 fine color reproductions by early Taos artists in this book.)

Hodge, Frederick W. *Handbook of the American Indian.* Pageant Press. 1960. Reprint. Bureau of American Ethnology, Bulletin 30. 2 Vols. 1907.

Jackson, Donald (editor). *The Journals of Zebulon Montgomery Pike.* University of Oklahoma Press, Norman, Oklahoma. 2 Vols. 1966.

Keleher, William. *The Maxwell Land Grant.* Rydal Press, Santa Fe, New Mexico. 1942. Reprint Argosy Antiquarian, New York City. 1964.

Lane, Lydia S. *I Married A Soldier.* Horn & Wallace. Reprint. 1964. (*"Army Life in the 1850's."* This is about Fort Burgwin and Kit Carson.)

Powell, J.W. United States Geological Survey, Director, *Twelfth Annual Report 1890-91 Part II Irrigation.* (Rio Grande Area and Taos County included.) This work available at libraries.

Rittenhouse, Jack D. *The Santa Fe Trail Bibliography.* University of New Mexico Press, Albuquerque, New Mexico. 1971.

Sanchez, George. *The Forgotten People.* University of New Mexico Press. Albuquerque, New Mexico. 1940. Reprint. Horn & Wallace, Albuquerque, New Mexico. 1967.

State Bureau of Mines and Mineral Resources, New Mexico. Institute of Mining and Technology, Socorro, New Mexico. *Number II Taos — Red River — Eagle Nest, New Mexico, Circle Drive, 1956.*

Thomas, E.B. (translator) *The Forgotten Frontiers.* Oklahoma Press, Norman, Oklahoma. 1932. (Journal of De Anza includes expedition through Taos Valley with 300 soldiers and 300 Indians after defeating Cuerno Verde, Comanche chief, at Rye, Colorado.)

Indian music and Spanish folksongs on disc records are available in Taos.

In this mad World — some things rather nice:
A drift of snow on sagebrush where winter birds rest.
The glow of sunset creeping across Taos Mountain.
Blue Lake lying quietly in the hearts of our neighbors —
Sacred, and eternally their own.
For these things, we can rejoice and be glad.

Liz Budlong — Taos
1970

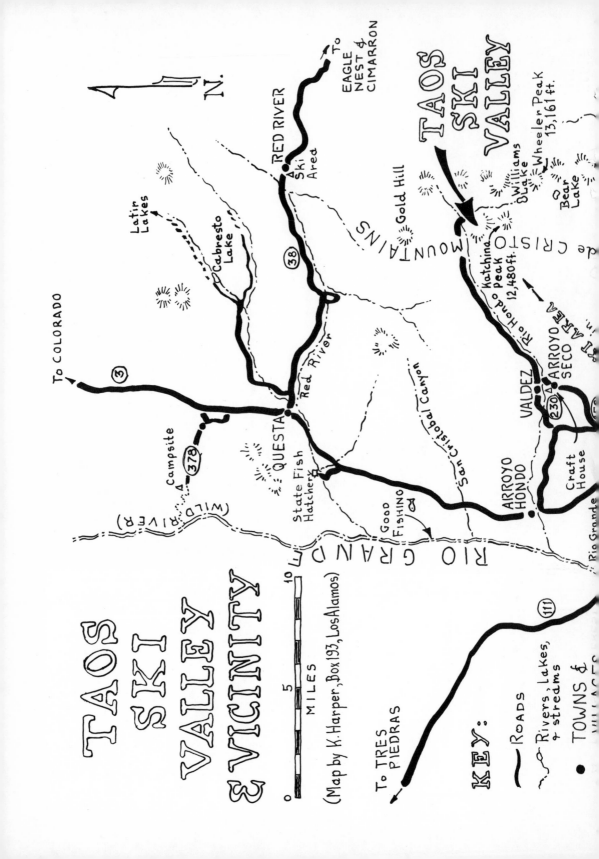